The Historian as Moralist
Reflections on the Study of
Tudor England

The John Coffin Memorial Lecture
1974

The Historian as Moralist
Reflections on the Study of Tudor England

by

JOEL HURSTFIELD

*Astor Professor of English History
in the University of London*

The John Coffin Memorial Lecture
delivered before the University of London
on 25th February 1974

UNIVERSITY OF LONDON
THE ATHLONE PRESS
1975

Published by
THE ATHLONE PRESS
UNIVERSITY OF LONDON
at 4 Gower Street London WC1

*Distributed by Tiptree Book Services Ltd
Tiptree Essex*

*U.S.A. and Canada
Humanities Press Inc
New Jersey*

© *University of London* 1975

ISBN 0 485 16209 1

*Printed in Great Britain by
Ebenezer Baylis and Son Ltd, Worcester*

The profession of historian is the second oldest in the world. Like the oldest profession it has always had a secure place in the entertainment industry. The television Tudors were, in the early 1970s, attracting larger audiences in one night of entertainment than the combined total of all the purchasers of the books written by Tudor historians since the war. I make this comparison with no intention of disparaging the work of television dramatists—or of Tudor historians—but simply to indicate the principal purpose which history serves for the majority of our fellow-countrymen; and in this it forms part of an ancient tradition.

From earliest times the minstrel historian in these islands would recall to prince and people the enthralling myths of their tribal past; and though they could not shorten the long northern winter they could at least make it a little easier to endure. The historian for many centuries remained essentially a storyteller whose resources consisted of the ever-extending mythology of his people. He was, secondly, a chronicler setting forth his narrative of events based in part on received traditions and in part on the experiences within his own life span. He could also recover something of a man's family history or, as a correspondent of Sir Thomas Dugdale put it, 'brush the dust from the tombs of their great-grandfathers'.[1] The historian was, thirdly, something of a priest and prophet trumpeting the greatness of his nation under the blessings of the gods, mourning its sufferings and losses when the gods were offended, and proclaiming the lessons which the past had to teach. Thus the priest and prophet was also a moralist.

But any process which glorifies the past, in the shape of

national achievement, religious purity, heroic endurance, or moral truths, sometimes imposes upon later generations ideals and objectives which restrain their freedom to develop and which shape, perhaps even determine, the pattern of their lives. Evidence of this may be seen today in Ireland, in Israel, and in many places on the American continent. The role of history which makes men prisoners of their past is a neglected subject to which I hope to return on another occasion. But, if historians have neglected it, dramatists have not. One of the most fascinating things about Shakespeare's plays is the recurrent pattern of man's tragic failure to escape from his past.

Yet if the historian is the custodian of the past he often has a special commitment to the present. We should never forget that, until comparatively recent times, the historian was the servant of the state who testified to its greatness, and this is still true in many places in the world. The best example I know of this in the past is Virgil's *Aeneid* where the poet-historian recites the glorious history of Rome culminating in the rise to power of the Emperor Augustus, in whose presence it was read. The climax where the historic process and the divine will combine to acknowledge Caesar is a masterpiece of poetic narrative and political propaganda:

> Hic vir, hic est, tibi quem promitti saepius audis,
> Augustus Caesar, Divi genus.[2]

I have often reflected on this passage in the *Aeneid* because it has helped me to understand the evolution of the Elizabethan myth. The assumption that God and history spoke with the same voice endowed the historian with an especial authority to expound political wisdom and moral truths. The historian as moralist thus came to assume one of his most characteristic postures.

The moral truths which we shall be considering in this

lecture are not concerned with private morality, an enormous subject in itself, but with the moral issues which arise in the actions of governments, that is, political morality. We shall in essence be examining the moral purposes attributed to governments, and the moral assumptions about the nature of government, in the writings of Tudor historians. I shall also try to show that, though later historians have rejected, or appeared to reject, the assumptions of their predecessors, they none the less write with moral assumptions which are sometimes explicit, but more often implicit, in their work. I shall not, of course, attempt to trace these developments from writer to writer, or generation to generation, but I shall examine some of the significant features in the evolution of the historian as moralist.

The historian lives in the present and the past. To do his work he has to acquire an almost schizophrenic condition of detached involvement. He is like an actor who plays Hamlet. A very great actor once told me that at each performance he suffered with Hamlet; otherwise, he said, 'I could not play the part.' 'But,' he added, 'I am at the same time detached from him, watching him at every step, trying to understand what is happening to him so that I can convey his experience to the whole theatre. Otherwise, again, I could not play the part.' This, it seems to me, is the problem of the historian.

I have often over the years tried to get into the mind and under the skin of Robert Cecil, minister of Elizabeth I and James I, that brilliant, crippled, corrupt, self-destructive man who enjoyed a concentration of power unparalleled since the time of Thomas Cromwell. I think that I have momentarily been able to sense what he felt, for example, when addressing a hostile House of Commons or was the target of the cruel pleasantries of Elizabeth I. I consider that compassion in the literal as well as the general sense is part of the necessary equipment of a biographer. But equally important is his independence, from the man and his age. Otherwise he will walk into the trap of condemning contemporaries who opposed the statesman and denigrating historians who had dissented from the judgment he is now putting forward. To adopt this viewpoint would be to become something of a public relations officer for a past government or minister. One might also be caught up in a long series of futile battles to defend an entrenched reputation, that of a dead politician or one's own.

The medieval monastic chronicler, however independent his researches, was a committed man, committed to the principles of his religion, to the traditions of his order and, in the last resort, to a personal loyalty to his house. It is scarcely an exaggeration to say that, until the later Middle Ages, most history in England was written by churchmen for churchmen. As a moralist, then, the historian's position was relatively simple. The evidence he examined, often the untested accounts of his predecessors, was placed against a scale of moral judgment which measured everything in terms of whether it conformed to Christian morality and brought good or ill to the church. Hence it is not surprising that King John received a bad press from the historian, became the archetypal 'bad king' and so remained for centuries until, with the coming of the Reformation, Foxe and Bale—understandably—found in King John a valiant defender of national independence against a usurping pope.[3] Yet, so powerful was the inherited tradition that twentieth century school-children are more familiar with John than with most medieval kings on the grounds that he signed Magna Carta (which he did not) and was a bad king (which is debatable). This does not mean that the best of medieval histories did not have an intrinsic value of their own. The successive authors of Bede's *Ecclesiastical History*, the *Anglo-Saxon*

Chronicle and other works provided important sources still essential for medieval scholars; but their horizon was limited by their calling.

That horizon was extended by many important developments in the fifteenth century, too well known and at the same time too complex to be discussed here. The readers of histories became more numerous and embraced a growing secular audience including country gentlemen but, more important, the educated and partially educated inhabitants of cities, especially London. The civic annal, beginning in some respects as a secularized version of the monastic chronicle, developed into a lively narrative and vigorous expression of urban pride.[4] And this is only one stage removed from the characteristic national history we associate with Polydore Vergil's *Anglica Historia* in the first half of the sixteenth century and, later on, with the work of Leland, Hall, Stow, Holinshed, and, in its most advanced form, with Camden's *Annals*.

It is not my intention to suggest that the sixteenth-century histories were merely monastic chronicles which had grown up in an urban environment. Historical methods, in the conditions of the Renaissance, had matured. There was much more of a critical testing of the sources rather than the acceptance of pious myths. But there was commitment, too, to civic and national pride, pride in the past as an inspiration for the future. And here it is important to remember that to Renaissance scholars the study of history was expected to continue into contemporary times in contrast with our own recent traditions that it should stop short of a man's own lifetime. To the scholars of the Renaissance, history had a certain immediacy but it therefore held certain perils, for they too, like their medieval predecessors, believed that history had lessons to teach.

In this context we naturally think of Machiavelli who in the early sixteenth century used historical evidence, in his *History of Florence*, to show how Italy could advance to nationhood, and in *The Prince*, to indicate how rulers could preserve their authority. Machiavelli was the first secular historian of the modern period in that the morals he was concerned with owed nothing to Christianity but were directed to the interests of the citizen and government in the emergent nation state. He believed passionately in the future greatness of Italy but he coolly explained to the prince not what he *should* do but what he would *need* to do if he wished to govern and maintain order. His aims and his use of his sources convinced generations of Englishmen that he was the personification of the worst Italianate vices—and the adjective Machiavellian remains a favourite term of abuse. Yet it was Francis Bacon who long ago saw that Machiavelli was a realist who examined human behaviour in a political context and, in a famous passage, thanked him for depicting not how men ought to behave but how, in fact, they do behave.[5] In spite of nearly five centuries of denunciation nobody, so far as I am aware, has ever shown that successful rulers behave profoundly differently from the description given by Machiavelli. 'The authentic interpreter of Machiavelli,' wrote Lord Acton, 'is the whole of later history.'[6] Someone like myself who spent the summer of 1973 in Washington fascinated by Watergate, and who in February 1974 is delivering the Coffin lecture in the middle of a quite extraordinary general election campaign, hesitates to reject the testimony of Machiavelli on how men acquire or use political power.

Polydore Vergil, like Machiavelli, was an Italian; but he was a priest who came to England as a papal collector in 1502, where he held various livings, at one time as Archdeacon of Wells. He was already an established author and, after a somewhat chequered period, settled down to his ecclesiastical duties and to historical research. His earliest English work was the first part of his *Anglica Historia*, dealing with events up to 1513, and completed in that year. At intervals thereafter the *History* was revised and extended; the last edition, published in 1555, the year of his death, carried the narrative to 1537, that is almost three-quarters of the way through Henry's reign.

Thanks to the major studies of Professor Denys Hay,[7] we can now see the powerful influence exercised by Polydore Vergil upon Tudor historiography. He skilfully analysed and criticized his sources and dissected some hallowed myths, of which the Arthurian legends were the most important examples. The legends he left as legends but his sceptical neutrality was sufficient to infuriate the stalwart defenders of a patriotic tradition. His scholarly standards were high yet, when he came to write of more recent times, his basic political moral became explicit. In brief, he saw in the Tudors the fulfilment of an historical process through war and disorder to unity, peace and good government. In his accounts of Henry VII and Henry VIII the role of an independent historian yielded place to that of a scholarly defender of the existing order; and historians writing on the Tudor period long afterwards did so with the powerful influence of Vergil's character studies still upon them.

Vergil finds in the workings of Providence an explanation of the triumph of Tudor rule. But Providence was not solely concerned with the English. It could on occasion intervene on behalf of the Italians, as in 1513 at the battle of Milan when the French lost 10,000 killed or captured. 'In this', writes Vergil, 'we can see that God always protects the innocent.'[8] Similarly at Flodden in 1513, Providence, along with a considerable number of troops, deserted the Scottish king and left him to a defeat he deserved.⁹ Providence and history teach by example: good government brings good results. Vergil, unlike his fellow countryman, Machiavelli, argues that good government can only be accomplished by good men. 'Princes', he tells us, 'should always rely solely on the services of honourable men.' Wolsey is a disastrous minister and represents the evil consequences of pride, ambition and greed.¹⁰

For all his devotion to historical research, Polydore Vergil wrote also as a moralist. It is perfectly possible, as we read through his *History*, to detect implied criticism of Tudor rule and open criticism of the governing classes, for example in their dealing with agricultural enclosures.¹¹ But this does not affect the central theme: Tudor kingship was established and survived because it deserved to.

The pattern set by Vergil was largely followed by later and better known historians among whom we may include Hall, Foxe, and Holinshed who, though they criticized him, were none the less influenced by his work. What Vergil, the Italian, implies Edward Hall states in the strident tones of a nationalistic, protestant Englishman.¹² The Tudor dynasty was the result of the union of the two houses of Lancaster and York, and Henry VIII was, as the sub-title of Hall's *Chronicle* says, 'the indubitable flower and very heir of both the said lineages'. The history of the fifteenth century, he showed, taught by example: usurpation brought civil war, civil war disrupted society and led to misery, murder and the destruction of the state. And now, an ancient prophecy was to be fulfilled with the coronation of the first Tudor

as a thing by God elected and provided and by his especial favour and gracious aspect compassed and achieved. Insomuch that men commonly report that seven hundred and ninety-seven years past it was by a heavenly voice revealed to Cadwallader, last king of the Britons, that his stock and progeny should reign in this land and bear dominion again.¹³

By God elected and provided and by his especial favour and gracious aspect compassed and achieved. Hall, writing in the same period as Polydore Vergil, has little of the Italian's restraint. God was in His Heaven and the Tudors were on the throne. Only another decade would have to pass before Englishmen could be told, on the high authority of John Aylmer, future Bishop of London, that

... you fight not only in the quarrel of your country but also and chiefly in defence of His [God's] true religion and of His dear son Christ.[14]

Granted this, it was not wholly unreasonable for Aylmer to write in the margin: 'God is English'[15]

Now that this was no longer doubt all the rest followed. Indeed, as we consider Aylmer's later career we get the impression not only that God was English but that he was Anglican, and high Anglican at that.

When John Foxe came to write his *Acts and Monuments* or, as it is better known, his *Book of Martyrs*, he could describe the history of his own time as a dramatic advance to the fulfilment of God's prophecy for a nation which had sought and recovered divine truth.[16] It was widely believed until recently that Foxe was a poor historian whose accounts were utterly untrustworthy;[17] but his facts have stood up remarkably well to the tests of modern scholarship.[18] And the epic pattern of his work made it a household book until the present century. Everyone is familiar with his account of the promise of the true religion under Henry VIII, blighted in the persecutions of his last years; the renewed prospects in the short reign of Edward VI, to be followed by the dark years of Mary, when the glorious martyrdom of nearly three hundred of the faithful proved that the light of God could not be put out. Foxe goes on to describe the fate of Mary and draws his moral:

Mark here, Christian reader, the woeful adversity of this queen, and learn withal what the Lord can do, when man's wilfulness will needs resist him, and will not be ruled.[19]

And all this leads to the accession of Queen Elizabeth. 'In speaking whereof', Foxe says disarmingly, 'I take not upon me the part here of the moral or of the divine philosopher, to judge of things done, but only keep me within the compass of historiographer declaring what hath been done before, and comparing things done with things now present, the like whereof, as I said, is not to be found lightly in chronicles before.'[20] There can be no doubt that Foxe had written a masterpiece: his pattern of Tudor England is the one which has survived, even in the text books of writers who have never read a line he wrote.

The faith expressed by Aylmer and Foxe about the future of England under Elizabeth seemed to be confirmed by the passing decades. Combining the offices of historians, moralists, and prophets they heralded a peaceful England in a warlike world. And now, in the middle of her reign, an eminent Italian visitor, Giordano Bruno, found here for a moment the prophecy fulfilled with the establishment of a most happy state:

The fortunate success of her reign is the wonder of the present age; for, whilst in the heart of Europe the Tiber runs angrily, the Po looks threatening, the Rhone rages with violence, the Seine is full of blood, turbulent is the Garonne, the Ebro and the Tagus pursue their course with fury, the Moselle is disturbed, and unquiet flows the Danube, she with the splendour of her eyes for the space of five lustres and more has tranquillised the great Ocean which peacefully receives into the ample ebb and flow of its vast bosom her dear Thames, . . .[21]

It was not unreasonable, therefore, that when Camden, Elizabeth's greatest historian, was invited, towards the end of her reign, to write its history, he saw it as a noble enterprise. Lord Burghley, the queen's principal adviser, had asked him to do so, offering him access to the state papers; and, he tells us, 'I obeyed him and not unwillingly, lest I might seem either to neglect the memory of that most excellent Princess, or to fail his expectation and (which I prized as dear as them both) the Truth itself.'[22]

His *Annals* of Elizabeth is still indispensable to students of the period and it aims at, and achieves, a large measure of impartiality in spite of the pressures upon him. It is relevant, therefore, to consider his methods as a historian, as he himself describes them.

... Things manifest and evident I have not concealed; things doubtful I have interpreted favourably; things secret and abstruse I have not pried into. 'The hidden meanings of Princes (saith that great Master of History) and what they secretly design to search out, it is unlawful, it is doubtful and dangerous: pursue not therefore the search thereof'. And, with Halicarnasseus I am angry with those curious, inquisitive people, who will needs seek to know more than by the laws is permitted them.[23]

What Camden set out to do he accomplished. It has been said for centuries that he modified his judgment of Mary, Queen of Scots to please James I; but as Professor Trevor-Roper has shown, Camden took care that the second part of his *Annals*, to be published posthumously, should be his independent judgment of events.[24] And there is throughout the book a remarkably tolerant spirit, an awareness that minority opinion cannot simply be ignored or condemned. He understands the position of Catholics in England and criticizes them, as did Lord Burghley, only on the basis of their affiliation to a foreign power—admittedly an over-simplification but significant in itself.[25] He is more bitter about the Puritans, whose extremism he recognizes as a threat to internal peace and order.[26] To the Earl of Leicester he is grossly unfair.[27]

Yet he is, if one may use the term, the most liberal of Tudor historians, as well as the most scholarly. But his scale of values is that which he himself sets before us in his Introduction.

As a historian Camden felt that he was the servant of the truth; but he saw himself also as a servant of the state. It is relevant therefore to compare his experiences when invited to write his Elizabethan history with what happened to Fulke Greville when he embarked without state patronage on the same enterprise. Greville tells us in his biography of his friend Philip Sidney that it had occurred to him to write a study of the queen herself. He therefore approached the Secretary of State, Robert Cecil—whose father Lord Burghley had opened the state papers for Camden—and asked for similar access. Cecil readily agreed and told Greville to come back in three weeks' time. When he returned Cecil half-jokingly enquired why he should waste his time 'in writing a story' when such a promising career lay ahead as a government servant. More pointedly Cecil asked whether his account of a past reign might not serve to show up the faults of the present age; and then, after further questioning, the minister said that he could do nothing in the matter unless he first obtained the king's permission. Greville at once saw that this would be followed by the censorship of what he wrote with 'sheet after sheet to be viewed', as he put it. He therefore abandoned his hope of getting to the documents and with it his plans for writing a biography of the queen.[28]

Fulke Greville was a poet, biographer, and dramatist, not a historian, but he had easily recognized the hazards. Sir Edward Coke was a lawyer (and, it must be admitted, not a very good historian) but he had great faith that through history men might discover the truth in politics: 'Best to ask counsel of the dead, for they will not flatter nor fawn to advance themselves, nor bribe nor dissemble

...'[29] But that eminent historian James I was ready to give short shrift to enquiry into historical precedent. 'I scorn to be likened to the times of some kings. Henry VI was a silly weak king. If you search precedents, look to the precedents of my time and of Queen Elizabeth, of Henry VIII, Henry VII, they are all good precedents...' Coke was warned personally not to use precedents against the king;[30] and it is no wonder that James I had no use for the Society of Antiquaries with its lively interest in medieval institutions. The great legal-historical controversy of the early seventeenth century turned mainly on medieval origins, not Tudor precedents, and falls outside of our consideration here.

By the time we come to the historical criticism by Coke and the legal antiquaries like John Selden we have come some distance from the basic pattern of Tudor historians. But before leaving the Tudor writers we may observe that their moral outlook is perhaps best summarized in the Elizabethan *Homily against Disobedience and Wilful Rebellion*:

Turn over and read the histories of all nations; look over the chronicles of our own country; call to mind so many rebellions of old time, and some yet fresh in memory; ye shall not find that God ever prospered any rebellion against their natural and lawful Prince, but contrariwise, that the rebels were overthrown and slain, and such as were taken prisoners dreadfully executed.[31]

I have embarked on this brief consideration of Tudor historiography because of its deep commitment to moral issues and because its approach, but not its methods, may still be detected in the work of modern scholars. But I have not in any way been concerned to evaluate individual writers of the sixteenth century in terms of their scholarship. I have no doubt that, in any age, men like Polydore

Vergil, Hall, Foxe, Camden would have established themselves in the front rank for their technical skill and creative literary powers. Nor have I considered great researchers like Leland or William Lambarde or John Stow, whose work was less in the main stream of the political historians I have just named, though their mastery of their sources, their devotion and discipline would have aroused admiration in any generation, including our own. I have been concerned with one single point: what political morals did Tudor historians teach? They taught that evil men were, sooner or later, punished by an avenging deity; they taught that England under the Tudors, with the exception of Mary, advanced towards an ordered, stable, civil society, strengthened and preserved by the true Protestant faith; and they taught that all forms of dissent sinned against Christ and his servant on earth, the Tudor prince. They enjoined conformity and sanctified the existing order.

It is understandable that the writers of the sixteenth century, deeply aware of the nature and consequences of civil war in this country and in Europe, anxious as to what would happen if the Tudor dynasty were overthrown, should, like their fellow Englishmen, rally to the existing order and write not only in its defence but morally justifying its authority and rule. I emphasize that they wrote this, not because they were told to but because they believed it. Yet we should also remember that this was an age when the control and creation of opinion was sought, and in some measure gained, by the government itself; that proclamations, statutes, homilies, officially sponsored pamphlets were aimed at forming and guiding opinion; that the Star Chamber and other branches of government censored the press and punished the deviants; that to be a practising Catholic or Protestant nonconformist invited severe penalties of restraint. Of course the restraints were sometimes thwarted and broken, of course there was criticism in speech and print. But the power of repression in most cases could silence the voice of dissent.

What happens in a controlled society when the historian, either through choice or by constraint, does not comment freely on the history of the recent past? If other experience provides any guide, alternative channels of communication are cut so that the movement of ideas and comment may continue. One such channel is developed by churchmen who reject the official version of the monarchy and state; another channel may be cut by dramatists.

The evidence we have examined so far has shown churchmen like Foxe and Aylmer (and there were many more) defending the established Protestant order as expressed and safeguarded in the monarchy of Elizabeth I. This kind of relationship between church and state is a familiar one and can be traced back to biblical times. But there is also a contrasting relationship and that too may find precedents in the Bible: it is based on the role of the church as critic. For if Christians are instructed to render unto Caesar the obedience due to him they also have a code of political morality which derives, not from Caesar, but from God as expounded by his prophets. As long as the exposition of the Bible rested with the ecclesiastical authorities under the jurisdiction of the papacy, collaboration—and conflict—between church and state were in the nature of collaboration and conflict between two authorities external to each other and operating from different power bases, the king representing secular power, the pope spiritual. It is true also that men like Thomas Becket were English churchmen who were, or had been, servants of the crown. But their ultimate source was in Rome. Individual conscience cut across both spheres; sometimes the idealist churchman, or the heretic, or the rebel recognized no such division of jurisdiction. But these were exceptional.

The Protestant Reformation, solvent of so much in state-church relationships, transformed the role of critic from being representative of an exterior power to one who presented an *internal* challenge laid at the roots of government itself. It is of great importance that at the same time there was a Catholic challenge to the Tudor monarchy, a challenge which at its best was that of idealists destined for martyrdom, of whom in their different ways Thomas More and Thomas Campion were noble exemplars. Other aspects of Catholic resistance, like that of Cardinal Allen and Robert Parsons, belong much more to the centuries-old conflicts between church and state. But in both cases the authority they looked to was still exterior to the king and the realm.

With the radical wing of protestantism, growing up within the Church of England itself, things were different. They looked neither to the papacy, nor to the Fathers, nor to the practice of the Church, all of which had been in a measure discredited during the formative decades of the Reformation. They looked instead to what they regarded as the traditional English Church and, above all, to the Bible. Where they challenged the crown they did so from within as loyal Englishmen, who were as Protestant as the queen. They, too, found the history of the people of Israel as full of relevant moral codes as did men like Foxe. But the codes were different for they learned from the Bible of the fallibility of kings who, when in error, had been overthrown by a righteous people guided by the infallible doctrine enshrined in the Word which God had made accessible to the faithful. I am not for one moment suggesting that the interpretation of the Bible in social and political terms bred revolutionaries, though the anabaptists of Munster in the 1530s served as a permanent warning to the governing classes of Europe. But what is clear is that henceforth the powers of the English monarchy could be questioned from within its own church and by men using those very sources, history and the Bible, on which the new and enlarged authority of the crown had been erected. Edmund Grindal was no revolutionary, but the highest ecclesiastical authority in England, under the queen. Yet in a famous letter to her he proclaimed that Christians owed obedience to a power superior to herself.[32] Thomas Cartwright likewise used the weight of his scholarship to question the exercise of the queen's authority. So, in different ways, did Members of Parliament, like Peter Wentworth and James Morris. So was it manifest in the robust polemics of Martin Marprelate.

In the late 1580s this questioning came in its most profound form in the works of radical separatists like Henry Barrow and John Greenwood. 'Whatsoever then is agreeable unto the word of God', wrote Barrow, 'is agreeable unto the state, and whatsoever is contrary unto the word of God is contrary unto the state.' Barrow is, for our purpose, the most interesting of the separatists for his case is simply stated and direct. The queen's authority, he says, is under God from whom all royal power is derived and to whom all monarchs must give account. Where there is a conflict between the laws of men and of God, then God rather than men has to be obeyed. He pours scorn on what he describes as blasphemous titles of papal origin such as Supreme Head of the Church.[33]

If in pamphlets and sermons an alternative view of history and political morality could be expressed, the theatre offered other platforms for dissent. I remain sceptical of the many examples given by scholars of specific, though disguised, comment by Shakespeare and his contemporaries on individual events and persons; but I am familiar with certain instances where the evidence appears to be strong. The point was not lost on the government, as its treatment of Ben Jonson and Samuel Daniel in the early seventeenth century makes clear. We know, too, that Shakespeare's play, *Richard II*, was used by the Essex faction, on the eve of their rebellion, to warn Elizabeth that monarchs could be overthrown—an incident which she herself bitterly commented upon in a famous interview with the historian Lambarde.[34] What as a historian I find fascinating in Shakespeare's plays is not simply social criticism of which there is plenty but the diversity of opinion expressed in them or, as I will put it, the moral neutrality of the plays. It is often said that Shakespeare was influenced by that combined enterprise known as *The Mirror for Magistrates*, with its interminable verses sometimes enshrining one-dimensional moral lessons.[35] But, in fact, when we turn from the *Mirror* to Shakespeare's plays we enter an entirely different world. Rebellion of course is suppressed, usurpation is punished, the birth of Elizabeth in the play *Henry VIII* (if indeed Shakespeare can be regarded as part author) represents the triumph of peace, order, and glory. But when that has been said we are still in a complex world in which, whatever the ultimate reward for virtue may be, the men who live out their lives in this world are the prey of injustice, evil and the blind strokes of fortune. Providence, in some conflicts, seems to be behaving like a neutral.[36] After all, what moral does *Hamlet* teach, or *King Lear*, or *Othello*, or *The Merchant of Venice*? It is this quality in his work which separates Shakespeare's approach from the simplistic morality of the historians, the homilists and the whole Establishment in church and state.

In the last decade a number of literary scholars have shown that Shakespeare had set himself free from the narrow providential theories—I almost say determinism—to be found in Holinshed; and Professor Moody Prior's new book, *The Drama of Power*, demonstrates amongst other things that Shakespeare 'subjected it [the idea of providence] to dramatic exploration which is at times shattering in exposing the absurdities of the idea as it is used in the chronicles'.[37] If this is true of the intervention of Providence in human affairs, it is equally true of the divinity of monarchy and its supremacy in politics. Precisely because they carried no consistent 'message' the plays were politically important in their display of moral diversity, in their erosion of the autonomous, self-perpetuating, political morality of the Tudors. In a controlled society the non-didactic theatre can sometimes make a greater contribution than a theatre of revolt for instead of directing a frontal assault on government policy and principles, which can easily be identified and suppressed, it can undermine the basic assumptions of the existing order. One of the uncovenanted contributions of a great dramatist is to make his audience aware that life is much more complex than the politicians would have us believe. In preserving diversity the dramatists, like the radical Protestants, did more than the historians to sustain some modicum of liberty in face of the expanding claims of the Tudor state.

When we come in the early seventeenth century to Francis Bacon we are conscious of a change in climate. He was not the first philosopher of science to see that its progress was inhibited by the cumbrous inheritance of Providence; and he played his part in liberating science from the inherited assumptions of the age. On the basis that it was presumptuous of man to try to understand and explain the ways of God, the First Cause, he banished divinity from the laboratory and made possible the freer exploration of natural phenomena. He was seeking to do much the same thing for history, resuming the work of Macchiavelli, though in an utterly different context and with wholly different aims. In his work there are times when he does indeed speak of the 'secret providence of God'.[38] But it is, in the main, analytical history, secular history at its best, and it marks in historiography both the closing of an old era and the opening of a new.

I do not propose to tarry long with the historians of the seventeenth and eighteenth centuries who wrote on Tudor England. There is, of course, greater freedom of comment. Within a year of her death, Sir Walter Ralegh was at his trial describing Elizabeth as a 'lady whom Time had surprised'[39] and shortly after he described her father Henry VIII as a tyrant.[40] Camden condemned Henry VIII outright;[41] indeed the king never recovered his early glory among the historians or politicians of this period though, as is well known, the reputation and charisma of Elizabeth was used as a stick to beat the early Stuarts. In the later seventeenth century, Strype[42] and Burnet,[43] both ecclesiastics, paid tribute to the Tudor achievement in church and state and, especially Strype, printed some valuable sources for studying the period. When David Hume came to write his history of England in the middle of the eighteenth century, his judgment on the Tudors is remarkably balanced. He saw Henry VIII as displaying 'violence, cruelty, profusion, rapacity, injustice, obstinacy, arrogance, bigotry, presumption, caprice' but he could also be 'sincere, open, gallant, liberal and capable at least of a temporary friendship and attachment'. However, Hume, as a less than neutral Scot, attributes the popularity of the king, in spite of his tyranny, to the fact that 'the English in that age were so thoroughly subdued that, like eastern slaves, they were inclined to admire those acts of violence and tyranny which were exercised over themselves, and at their own expense'.[44] For Elizabeth, Hume displayed the greatest admiration. He saw her as one of the greatest monarchs to sit on any throne and he found her in complete control of the political situation, with her statesmen in effect her servants. Though she lived before the age of toleration she had, he argues, a remarkably moderate approach to religious faction. He sighs that she seems to have too little of some womanly qualities such as 'softness of disposition, some greater lenity of temper, some of those admirable weaknesses by which her sex is distinguished'; but adds that though we might not fancy her as a wife or mistress we could not fail to admire her as a sovereign.[45]

It is interesting to compare the views of Hume, the Scottish rationalist, writing in the middle of the eighteenth century, with those of Froude, the English historian writing in the middle of the nineteenth. We may consider first Froude's views on history as set out in his inaugural lecture to the Regius Chair of Modern History at Oxford.

An inaugural lecture is, I am aware, a doubtful source. It is often the first fine careless rapture of the new professor when he presents grandiose schemes of work to be carried through during his tenure of the Chair to a somewhat sceptical audience, some of whom hope to live until his retirement when they will have the bizarre pleasure of comparing his promise with his performance. But when Froude delivered his inaugural he was already 74 years of age and it must have seemed to him a little late in the afternoon to present too extravagant a series of proposals for the work ahead. Instead his inaugural became something of a valedictory as he surveyed what he had done. He also commented on the nature of history itself:

I cannot teach a philosophy of history (he wrote) because I have none of my own. Theories shift from generation to generation and one ceases to believe in any of them. I know nothing of, and I care nothing for, what are called the laws of development, evolution or devolution, extension of constitutional privileges from reign to reign, to end in no one knows what. I see in history only a stage on which the drama of humanity is played by successive actors from age to age.[46]

Old men forget. Far from displaying no philosophy of history his magnificent twelve-volume study, the *History of England from the fall of Wolsey to the defeat of the Spanish Armada*[47] is in effect a consistent and powerful plea to his fellow countrymen to learn the moral of Tudor England in the crisis which faced them in the mid-nineteenth century. To Froude, Victorian England, passing through what looked like a major Catholic revival, was in danger of losing its whole character. The completion of this process would mean the end of both the freedom and the national independence of England. Hence the importance of the Tudor epoch: and the moral? That England was at her greatest under Henry VIII and again under Elizabeth, two national protestant princes (though he thought that Elizabeth owed most of her strength to Burghley), and at her weakest under Mary when the power of the priest was restored. In essence, Froude recalled his own generation to re-live the Tudor experience, so that history might prove the instrument of national re-awakening and restored power. And so national independence was a kind of secular Providence which rewarded those people who were faithful to her trust.

If my all too summary account is correct, the historian as moralist, though he had discarded the supernatural machinery which was the stock in trade of sixteenth-century writers, still showed that the preservation of national unity and strength was the political moral which each generation must learn and apply, and to which each generation must submit. Even the Whig historians like S. R. Gardiner, while writing scathingly about the tyranny of Henry VIII and his minister, Thomas Cromwell, were prepared to acknowledge that strong government was what the times had required. But it was Gardiner who put the problem in its larger moral perspective.

The Government (he said) was all-powerful to suppress generally recognised abuses, but its power was not always limited to such beneficial exercises of authority. Injustice was often done, sometimes from ignorance of the principles of political morality, and sometimes because the hostility of the Government was directed against an unpopular object. The nation was capable of supporting measures which were in themselves essentially unjust, and it was more than probable that it would frequently be desirous of obtaining justice by unjust proceedings. Still more frequently it would look on in silence whilst injustice was done to individuals whose wrongs were not of a nature to provoke any general resistance.[48]

He dismissed in a few sentences the view, still widely held, that this was government by consent because people did not rebel. Moreover, Gardiner put his finger on a point which some later historians have yet to accept: that the popular support of a tyrannical regime does not automatically make it good. *Vox populi* is not necessarily *vox dei*.

An English population would hardly resist an obnoxious Government, unless their grievances were of such a nature as to be felt by large masses. Individual cases of tyranny would not therefore move them to rebellion, however much they might sympathise with the sufferers.[49]

A. F. Pollard came closer than any of his predecessors to an understanding of Henry VIII, in his biography written at the beginning of this century. It may be that his own experience of how men behave in the world of politics sharpened his judgment for, in spite of his admiration for the king, Pollard did not accept his moral statements at their face value. He saw that Henry's addiction to the forms of law was no proof of his respect for justice, least of all when it was sought by minority, dissenting opinion. But Pollard also claimed that the majority of Tudor Englishmen were no more concerned with the issues of liberty than was the king. Hence—'The indifference of his subjects to political issues tempted Henry along the path to tyranny, and despotic power developed in him features, the repulsiveness of which cannot be concealed by the most exquisite art, appealing to the most deep-rooted prejudice'.[50]

In saying this Pollard may have been right. It is often said that most people set greater store by security, comfort, and a square meal than they do by liberty of conscience in any abstract sense. But it is also true that most men want to be left alone, free from the dominance of their masters in the capital; and this seems to have been true even in the sixteenth century. Yet, Pollard argued, it was the very ruthlessness of the king who 'took his stand on efficiency rather than principle', which saved England from the turbulence of the Reformation struggles and which made the story of Tudor London so different from that of Valois Paris. So Pollard himself applied the political test that the preservation of the state was the supreme moral first cause. But he was a liberal, too, and he took his full measure of the king.[51]

If some of the things that Gardiner and Pollard said reflected the liberal outlook of their time, they showed the marks also of profound changes taking place in the conditions and profession of the historian. Many of those who had written the history of Tudor England hitherto had been drawn from various walks of life, ecclesiastics like Strype and Burnet, philosophers like Hume, men of letters like Froude. History was either their avocation or it was their profession, that is, they made their living by selling their books. But it was not an academic profession, they were not writing within the university and training students. Froude did not become an academic until the end of his life. But, on the other hand, both Gardiner and Pollard were professors in the University of London; and we notice that from now on an increasing proportion of the works on the Tudor period is written by academics. Another change during the nineteenth century was at least as important. It was the opening up of the records of government in all their abundance to modern scholars; and the calendars, indexes, and guides to official records provided marvellous keys to this great treasury. Of course, historians since the time of Camden, and before that, had used official sources but amidst all the handicaps of poor depositories, little information about materials and the lonely search through a wilderness in which no path had been cleared. It is all the more remarkable that Froude accomplished what he did in the records of this country, Spain and elsewhere, with a close and detailed reading of his sources to a degree which showed him vastly superior to his critics.

But government records are government records. It was, of course, natural that the emphasis in academic writing and research moved increasingly in the direction of government and, more especially, administration; and university shelves in this country and the United States began to be filled with Ph.D. dissertations in these fields of study. At their best they could provide ideal training for the young historian; but at their worst, if the student looked at matters primarily from the government standpoint, they could narrow the scope, dull the vision, sterilize the imagination, and create notions of self-importance in their authors. Apart from this they also created an illusion. For it seemed that now at last the historian was set free from the value judgments of his predecessors and could write detailed studies of government which took a cool, independent, almost scientific view of the state: history, it would appear, had set itself free from moral commitment.

That this is an illusion will be manifest to anyone who studies the historiography of Henry VIII and Thomas Cromwell in the present century. Nowadays moral judgments are rarely explicit. We no longer speak of good or bad kings or provide a descending order of merit for statesmen. But our judgments are implicit; and it is extraordinarily interesting to observe the pattern of judgment which can be detected equally well in the major work of scholarship as in the elementary school text book. It is as follows. England in the first half of the sixteenth century was passing through a crisis in which her government could be overthrown and disorder prevail. Henry VIII, though tyrannical in many ways, sought to preserve unity and internal peace; his minister, Thomas Cromwell, variously depicted as a crude ruffian or a Machiavellian or a man of vision, was his able instrument in a patriotic cause. King and minister, though sometimes harsh, governed with the consent of the people; and this is proved by the fact that the government survived without a standing army; that there were no successful rebellions; and Parliament gave consent on behalf of the whole nation. Therefore the policies of Cromwell were morally right in principle and execution. We hear once more the voice of a secular Providence.

It is easy to understand how such a view can prevail; yet it ignores so much. It ignores the practice of the government in acting *in terrorem*, which Thomas Cromwell had mastered; it ignores the use of levies and mercenaries since no standing army existed; it makes no allowance for the powerful control of propaganda by the government and its suppression of dissenting opinion. For Tudor governments, or modern historians, to say that the people supported the government when it was hard for people to hear or express alternative views is to be caught in a circular argument. Most people could only reflect back to the government the views they were allowed to hear so that, to use a Tudor phrase, the government was playing tricks with mirrors.

I will exemplify this by only a few brief excerpts. For example, in a valuable book on the Reformation Parliament, Professor S. H. Lehmberg writes: 'In the Upper House as in the Lower, the parliamentarians gave effective voice to the sentiments of their countrymen.'[52] But how can one know that the parliamentarians expressed 'the sentiments of their fellow countrymen'? Here is Professor Lehmberg's own account of the last stage in the passing of the Act in conditional restraint of annates in 1532 (described by the ambassador, Chapuys, as a novel procedure): 'Henry ordered the members who would stand for his success and the welfare of the realm to one side of the House and those who opposed the measure to the other. Several who had earlier been in opposition joined the "yeas" for fear of the king's indignation, and a majority was obtained.'[53] How effectively, in such circumstances, could parliamentarians give voice to the sentiments of their countrymen. I prefer here the criticism which Professor A. G. Dickens applied to Pollard's views on the history of the Reformation, namely, he (Pollard) 'tended to equate the House of Commons with the English people'.[54]

In a recent book Professor A. J. Slavin tells us that 'The *final* overthrow of Lancastrian government resulted not from a conspiracy against it but from the judgment of the country.'[55] By what process of historical reasoning has Professor Slavin managed to equate force of arms with 'the judgment of the country'? And Professor G. R. Elton (who knows more about Tudor administrative processes than any man alive) speaks thus of Henry VIII's treatment of Thomas More: 'Though the King throughout displayed his animus against a man who, as he saw it, had betrayed both trust and friendship, the behaviour of a government forced by political circumstances into a thoroughly unhappy and bad decision was scrupulous rather than tyrannical.'[56] One must at once acknowledge that Professor Elton has on numerous occasions replied to those who criticize his concept of the Tudor state; but the basic issue of the distinction between law and justice has never been met. For, when all has been said, the cited passage, and especially the expressions 'forced by political circumstances' and 'scrupulous rather than tyrannical', blunt the issue by obscuring its moral content. The contrast between scrupulous and tyrannical is, in this context, an unreal one. Throughout history, and on into our own day, many authoritarian governments were, like Henry VIII, both scrupulous *and* tyrannical. We are therefore back at the *raison d'état* of Renaissance statesmanship. I do not deny, and never have denied, that Tudor England needed strong, centralized government. But I would do less than justice to both Thomas Cromwell and Thomas More if I did not also point out that this was a time when consent to legislation was often engineered and controlled, when men of noble spirit were destroyed and when freedom was repressed. To argue that an action cannot be tyrannical if it is sanctioned by law is to ignore the fundamental question of how laws are made. I will neither praise the government nor pour scorn on its opponents but it is right to point out that in those days—as of course in our own—men were faced with the moral issues of freedom and authority.

REFLECTIONS ON THE STUDY OF TUDOR ENGLAND 33

We have come a long way in this lecture from the time when a young Italian cleric, Polydore Vergil, landed in this country and wrote our history; and it may be that I have travelled too far and too fast. Yet my theme is a simple one: that most historians who have written the political history of Tudor England—I exclude economic and administrative history though not diplomatic history—most historians have expressed or implied moral judgments about the state, its power and its relation to individual liberty. But I have suggested that the historian's task is neither to condemn nor defend governments of the past but to ask among other questions how much freedom was there, how was consent obtained, by what criteria did rulers rule? I suggested, too, that the historian should aim at a detached involvement in the man or the government or the society he studies. He should feel as Hamlet felt yet should not be committed to the moral assumptions by which Hamlet lived. Nor should he look down from on high on Hamlet and his opponents, bestowing praise here, a curt condemnation there. In other words, though the historian may be able to play Hamlet, he can never play God. Those who have tried have not made much of a success of it.

Lord Acton never wrote his projected *History of Liberty*.[57] No-one else has written it, perhaps no one ever will. But at least historians could tell us something, for example, about the issues of liberty in the period they study. To write massive volumes on a past age and its government without even raising the question of freedom seems to me to treat historical technology as though it were history itself. It is, as it were, to say:

> For forms of government let fools contest,
> Whate'er is best administered is best.[58]

I would not advocate, as Lord Acton did, that historians should make moral judgments but that they should be sensitive to, and enquire into, moral issues of the past. For it is because of moral issues—not just obstinacy or stupidity—that men sometimes are in conflict with those in power.

History, as we understand it today, is the independent study of men, over a period of time, in their relations to government and society. The historian is always confronted with problems of liberty, authority, justice, consent, corruption, issues which are brilliantly explored by Professor Hugh Trevor-Roper, in his book *Religion, the Reformation and Social Change*.[59] But these enquiries in general are only in their beginnings. Yet if we take for example political corruption, it is too political to be left to the politicians alone, too socially complex to be left to the lawyers alone, too historical to be left to the sociologists alone. The historian too has a contribution to make, enlarged and illumined by the longer perspective of time and diversity of experience. In this context the historian can contribute to the instructed judgment of the educated citizen. For if these issues of freedom and authority confronted Englishmen in the sixteenth century, they stand out, too, as the great issues of our own day upon whose resolution the survival of our society may depend.

NOTES

1. Cited by C. R. Cheney in *English Historical Scholarship* in the sixteenth and seventeenth centuries, ed. L. Fox (1956) p. 3. I acknowledge with thanks the help of Mr Kenneth Powell, who was my research assistant in the session 1973-4.
2. *Aeneid*, Bk VI, ll, 791f.
3. J. Bale, *King John*, reprinted in *Elizabethan History Plays*, ed. W. A. Armstrong (1965); John Foxe, *Acts and Monuments* of these latter and perillous dayes, touching matters of the Church, first edition, Strasbourg, 1559 (commonly known as the *Book of Martyrs*).
4. See, for example, L. B. Wright, *Middle Class Culture in Elizabethan England* (2nd ed. 1958); F. J. Levy, *Tudor Historical Thought* (San Marino, Calif., 1967) esp. ch. VI and VII; May McKisack, *Medieval History in the Tudor Age* (Oxford, 1971).
5. *The Works of Francis Bacon*, ed. J. Spedding, R. L. Ellis and D. D. Heath (new ed. 1889) Philosophical Works, i. 729.
6. See Acton's Introduction to *Il Principe*, ed. L. A. Burd (Oxford, 1891) pp. xix-xx.
7. Denys Hay, *Polydore Vergil*, Renaissance historian and man of letters (Oxford, 1952); *The Anglica Historia of Polydore Vergil*, A.D. 1485-1537, ed. and trans. by Denys Hay (Camden Soc. 3rd ser. vol. lxxiv, 1950).
8. ibid., p. 207.
9. ibid., pp. 219ff.
10. ibid., p. 163 and *passim*.
11. ibid., pp. 277ff.
12. Edward Hall, *The Vnion of the two noble and illustre famelies of Lancastre and Yorke* (ed. Henry Ellis, 1809 as Hall's *Chronicle*).
13. ibid., p. 423.
14. John Aylmer, *An Harborowe for faithfull and trewe subjects* (Strasbourg, 1559) sig. P. 4 V.
15. ibid., loc. cit., marginal note.
16. Foxe's *Acts and Monuments*, first published in Strasbourg in 1559, ran through five editions in the Elizabethan period, 1563, 1570, 1576, 1583, 1596.
17. See e.g. J. Gairdner, *Lollardy and the Reformation in England* (1908-13) i. 333-65.

18. J. F. Mozley, *John Foxe and his Book* (1940); W. Haller, *Foxe's 'Book of Martyrs' and the elect nation* (1963).
19. *Acts and Monuments*, ed. S. R. Cattley and G. Townsend (1837–41) viii, 628.
20. ibid., p. 672.
21. As cited in Frances A. Yates, *Giordano Bruno and the Hermetic Tradition* (1964) p. 292.
22. William Camden, *The History of the most renowned and victorious Princess Elizabeth* (1688 ed.)—commonly known as Camden's *Annals*—Preface.
23. ibid., loc. cit.
24. H. R. Trevor-Roper, *Queen Elizabeth's First Historian* (1971) pp. 30ff.
25. *Annals*, pp. 271f.
26. ibid., pp. 420f.
27. ibid., pp. 419f.
28. Fulke Greville, *The Life of the renowned Sir Philip Sidney*, ed. Nowell Smith (Oxford, 1907) pp. 215ff. For a discussion of the relationship between Greville and Robert Cecil, Earl of Salisbury, see R. A. Rebholz, *The Life of Fulke Greville* (Oxford, 1971) *passim*.
29. *Commons Debates, 1621*, ed. W. Notestein, F. H. Relf and H. Simpson (1938) v. 414. I owe this, and the following reference, to my former student, Dr Joan Kent.
30. *Notes of the Debates in the House of Lords . . . 1621, 1625, 1628*, ed. Frances Helen Relf (Camden Soc. 3rd ser. xlii, 1929) p. 14.
31. *The Two Books of Homilies*, ed. J. Griffiths (Oxford, 1859) p. 579, cited in E. M. W. Tillyard, *The Elizabethan World Picture* (1943) p. 69.
32. *The Remains of Edmund Grindal*, ed. W. Nicholson (1843) pp. 376ff.
33. *The Works of Henry Barrow, 1587–90*, ed. L. H. Carlson (1962) p. 241 and *passim*.
34. Cited in J. E. Neale, *Queen Elizabeth* (1934) p. 381.
35. For a modern edition see *The Mirror for Magistrates*, ed. L. B. Campbell (Cambridge, 1938).
36. I discuss aspects of this question in my forthcoming 'The Politics of Corruption in Shakespeare's England' (*Shakespeare Survey*, ed. K. Muir, xxviii.
37. Moody E. Prior, *The Drama of Power* (Evanston, Ill., 1973) p. 356 (n. 10 to p. 58).
38. Cited in F. Smith Fussner, *The Historical Revolution* (1962) p. 269.
39. E. Edwards, *The Life of Sir Walter Ralegh* (1868), i, 398.

NOTES

40. W. Ralegh, *History of the World* (1687 ed.) pp. viiif.
41. W. Camden, op. cit., Preface.
42. J. Strype, *Annals of the Reformation* (Oxford, 1824 ed.) see especially ii, pp. ivf.
43. G. Burnet, *History of the Reformation* (Oxford, 1845 ed.) iii, 462f.
44. David Hume, *History of England* (1841 ed.) iii, 231.
45. ibid., iv, 188f.
46. J. A. Froude, 'Inaugural Lecture', *Longman's Magazine* (1892) xxi, 162.
47. First edition, 1856–70.
48. S. R. Gardiner, *History of England*, 1603–16 (1863) i, 34. This passage is in the first edition but not in that of 1883 where the early part is abbreviated.
49. ibid., i, 34 n.
50. A. F. Pollard, *Henry VIII* (1930 ed.) p. 438.
51. ibid., pp. 439f.
52. S. H. Lehmberg, *The Reformation Parliament* (Cambridge, 1970) p. 63.
53. ibid., pp. 137f.
54. Introduction to Pollard's *Henry VIII* (New York, 1966) p. xxi.
55. A. J. Slavin, *The Precarious Balance* (New York, 1973) p. 77.
56. G. R. Elton, *Policy and Police* (Cambridge, 1972) p. 419.
57. Cf. *D.N.B.*, 2nd Supplt. (1901–11) *sub* Acton.
58. Alexander Pope, *An Essay on Man*, Epistle III, 11.303f.
59. H. R. Trevor-Roper, *Religion, the Reformation and Social Change* (1967, 2nd ed. 1972).